BOOK ANALYSIS

Written by Natacha Cerf and Pauline Coullet

Translated by Rebecca Neal

AF131422

Thérèse Raquin
BY ÉMILE ZOLA

ÉMILE ZOLA

FRENCH WRITER AND JOURNALIST

- **Born in Paris in 1840.**
- **Died in Paris in 1902.**
- **Notable works:**
  - *Nana* (1880), novel
  - *The Ladies' Paradise* (1883), novel
  - *Germinal* (1885), novel

Émile Zola was born in 1840 and died in 1902. He is considered to be one of the greatest French novelists of the 19th century. He was also the leading figure of naturalism, a movement which sought to apply the experimental scientific methods of the time to literature: after observing reality, Zola would put forward a hypothesis and test it through experimentation in his books. This aesthetic can be seen in particular in *Les Rougon-Macquart*, a cycle of 20 novels which constitutes his most important work and met with major success, in spite of many criticisms.

Zola was also famous for his social and political stances, which often gave rise to condemnation. The best-known of these concerns the Dreyfus affair; his pamphlet *J'accuse* ("I accuse") had a major influence on the pardoning of the Jewish officer Alfred Dreyfus (1859-1935).

THÉRÈSE RAQUIN

A STORY OF PASSION AND DEATH

- **Genre:** novel
- **Reference edition:** Zola, É. (2013) *Thérèse Raquin*. Trans. Thorpe, A. London: Vintage.
- **1st edition:** 1867
- **Themes:** naturalism, the body, madness, animality, crime, investigation, vice

Thérèse Raquin was published in 1867 and was Zola's first great success as a novelist. In it, he puts his theory of naturalism into practice and tells the story of how Thérèse and her lover Laurent are driven to crime by the determinism of their bodies. The novel depicts the fear, suffering and hatred which follow murder and lead inexorably to the suicide of the two criminal lovers.

It is a novel in a new style, which broke with the literary tradition according to which all stories must contain psychology, heroes and a moral. This explains why the author was accused of writing pornography and described as unwholesome and corrupt. Nonetheless, *Thérèse Raquin* remains one of Zola's most memorable novels.

SUMMARY

When her mother, who was African, died, Thérèse was adopted by Madame Raquin. In spite of her excellent health, the young girl was treated as if she were as sickly as her cousin, Camille, and shared his bedroom and medicine throughout her entire childhood. This gave her the habit of repressing her fiery temperament. When they were old enough, Madame Raquin arranged for Thérèse to marry Camille.

After the wedding, Camille wanted to leave Vernon to go live in Paris, so his mother bought a small, gloomy shop in the Passage du Pont-Neuf. Thérèse loathed the dark and dilapidated shop. Every day she would collapse behind the counter, spending hours completely motionless, and every evening she would lie down next to her husband "contemptuously indifferent" (p. 7).

For three years, the daily life of the Raquins remains more or less the same. Thérèse, crushed by boredom, "saw life stretching out in front of her, totally bare, leading every evening to the same cold bed and every morning to the same empty day" (p. 18). Every Thursday evening, the Raquins are visited by the old police commissioner Michaud, his son Olivier and his wife Suzanne, as well as Grivet, an elderly employee of the Orléans railway.

One day, Camille brings Laurent into the shop. Laurent is

a childhood friend who has a heavy, calm appearance: "At bottom, he was a sluggard, with a full-blooded appetite, a fixed desire for easy, lasting enjoyment" (p. 25). He used to be a mediocre painter with a peasant's coarse eye, and he suggests painting Camille's portrait.

CHAPTERS VI-X

From then on, Laurent spends almost every evening at the Raquins' apartment. He starts working on Camille's portrait in a bedroom that has been turned into a studio. Thérèse watches him feverishly: "The sanguine nature of this fellow, his big voice, his heavy laughter, the strong and pungent odour which his body gave off troubled the young woman and threw her into a state of nerves" (p. 28). Thérèse, who has never experienced passion, is hopelessly attracted to this force of nature. Laurent realises the emotional turmoil he causes in Thérèse. They quickly become lovers ("Not a word passed between them. The act was silent and brutal", p. 32).

For eight months, the two lovers live "in a state of utter bliss" (p. 45). Thérèse finally has an outlet for her nervous temperament and all-consuming passion. Laurent, for his part, both loves and fears his lover's animality. He also makes the most of the Raquins' hospitality and friendliness: he is "sated, pampered and fattened up" (ibid.). However, as he has taken too much time off work, he is now forbidden from leaving early or he will be dismissed. The fact that it is difficult for the two lovers to see each other heightens their passion. Laurent realises "how necessary this woman had become to him" (p. 46). Without him noticing it, "his mistress, with her she-cat suppleness, her nervous pliancy, had insinuated herself little by little into every fiber of his body. He needed this woman as you need food and drink" (p. 47). They hatch the idea of murdering Camille.

CHAPTERS XI-XV

One Sunday, Camille, Thérèse and Laurent leave for Saint-Ouen. Laurent suggests taking a rowing boat out on the water. Once they are far from the shore, he pushes Camille out of the boat, which he then capsizes in order to fake an accident. Camille drowns, and his body is not found until much later. The police investigation rules that his death was an accident.

Laurent decides to identify Camille's body at the morgue himself so that his death can be made official and he can put an end to the matter. As the body has been in the water for 15 days, it has started to decompose and looks grotesque.

CHAPTERS XVI-XX

Laurent is haunted by the spectre of Camille, and spends the night stricken by terror. Thérèse suffers the same torment: every night, they are so anxious that they cannot sleep. They decide to convince Madame Raquin to support their marriage, hoping that once they are married, they will no longer be troubled by the drowned man.

The lovers' act eventually pays off. Michaud puts the idea of Laurent and Thérèse's marriage into Madame Raquin's head, and the two are soon married.

CHAPTERS XXI-XXV

The wedding night proves painful. Now, the only thing keeping them together is the horror of Camille's murder. The nights that follow are even more terrifying. After their wedding, Thérèse and Laurent's suffering deepens: their attempts to drive the drowned man from their bed by embracing one another and returning to their past desires fail: "it had been impossible to drive him from the bed; they were beaten" (p. 145).

Laurent rents a studio in order to get back to painting. He meets an old schoolfriend who praises his artistic sense. However, he points out that there is something similar about all of his paintings. Indeed, Laurent had never realised that the faces of all the people he paints look like Camille: their lips are twisted and pulled to one corner of their mouths, mimicking Camille's expression when his body was found. As he cannot fight his hand, which can do nothing but draw the drowned man again and again, Laurent decides to stop painting.

CHAPTERS XVI-XXX

Madame Raquin, devastated by her son's death, ages prematurely: she loses the ability to move and speak. The lovers' constant arguments gradually reveal to her the terrible truth hidden behind the façade of their apparent marital happiness. She understands everything and, imprisoned in her own body, sinks into a deep sadness: "Now all that was left for her was to die, denying love, denying friendship, denying devotedness. Nothing existed but murder and lust" (p. 170).

She gathers all that is left of her strength to denounce Laurent and Thérèse one Thursday evening, in front of their friends, by trying to trace the letters on the table. However, her strength runs out halfway through the sentence, so she cannot get her message across, and the other guests think that she was trying to say "Thérèse and Laurent take good care of me" (p. 176).

CHAPTERS XXXI-XXXII

After trying everything they can think of to escape this life of anguish and horror, Thérèse and Laurent once again end up face to face with one another, consumed by hatred and mistrust. They constantly threaten to turn the other person in, which ends up making them suspicious. Neither of them let the other out of their sight, out of fear that one of them will talk. As this constant closeness is unbearable, they each have the idea of killing the other to find peace. To do this, Laurent steals a flask of prussic acid from a friend who is a chemist's assistant, while Thérèse sharpens a kitchen knife. Just as she is about to grab the knife, Laurent pours the contents of the flask into a glass of sugared water. They both sense danger and turn to each other, understanding at that moment what they are both getting ready to do. They burst into tears. They are broken and decide to commit suicide by drinking the poison.

CHARACTER STUDY

THÉRÈSE RAQUIN

Thérèse is the daughter of a French captain named Degans and an African mother, from whom she has inherited her nervous, and perhaps even hysterical, temperament. She is the character who has the most decisive influence on the events of the novel.

She is adopted by Madame Raquin when her mother dies and, even though she is excellent health, she receives the same medical treatments as her sickly cousin. Forced to live like an invalid, she represses all her energy and spirit, and can only express them on rare occasions ("When she was alone, on the grass by the water's edge, she would lie flat on her front like an animal, eyes black and wide, body twisted, ready to leap", p. 11).

Her upbringing teaches her the art of hypocrisy. She is capable of a great deal of self-control: she conceals her true, quick-tempered nature behind a peaceful façade. She is a complicated woman who is capable of duplicity. Her calm, restrained expression conveys gentle indifference.

Her early years are marked by deference, self-denial and obedience. However, her unhappy marriage drives her into Laurent's arms. He pulls her out of her profound boredom and triggers a violent awakening of her numbed feelings:

> "This advance from a powerful man gave her a sudden jolt that wrenched her flesh from its long slumber. All the ins-

> tincts of a highly strung woman exploded with unparalleled violence; her mother's blood, that African blood burning in her veins, began to flow, to beat furiously in her lean, still all but virgin body" (p. 34).

Thérèse plays an essential role in the plot: she refuses to break off her relationship with Laurent when they can no longer see each other, and is the first person to hint at the idea of the crime. The murder which haunts her then leads her to a series of pathetic actions and reveals her monstrous nature. She develops a "nervous sensitivity" (p. 90) because she thinks that Camille is haunting her. She has an increasing number of nervous breakdowns and moments of terror. She can no longer stand to be around Laurent, because he reminds her of the drowned man.

At the end of the novel, her nerves have failed her. She has had enough of this life and dreams of killing Laurent so that she can finally be at peace. This peace only comes with her own death.

LAURENT

Laurent works at the Orléans train station and is brought to the Raquins' apartment by his childhood friend Camille. He soon becomes Thérèse's lover.

He is the son of a peasant farmer, and has large, square shoulders and the face of someone who knows how to enjoy life. His fresh, ruddy handsomeness fascinates Thérèse, who admires his thick neck and his large, powerful hands. He is completely dominated by his instincts and his hot-headed temperament. He is a brutal, animal-like man who lacks intelligence.

He waits for his father to die so that he can inherit his fortune. He is lazy and wants a selfish life of easy pleasures and peace. He is also calculating:

> "Thérèse was ugly, and he did not love her, but [...] she would cost him nothing. [...] As it was, thrift counselled him to take his friend's wife. Moreover, he had not gratified his appetites for a long time; money being scarce, he was depriving his flesh, and had no desire to let slip an opportunity to offer it a little nourishment" (p. 31).

His mistress becomes indispensable to him. Their hot-headed and nervous temperaments are perfectly suited to one another.

The breakdown of his nerves and his inability to forget Camille's murder drive him mad. He is disgusted with himself and ends up committing suicide.

CAMILLE RAQUIN

Camille, aged 30, is the only son of Madame Raquin and inspires disgust in other people. His body still bears the consequences of his sickly youth ("He was small and puny, with a listless manner, his hair an insipid blond, his beard sparse, face covered in freckles, he resembled a spoilt, sick child", p. 6). He is not intelligent and can do no better than a lowly positon at the Orléans railway company. He has many character flaws: his selfishness, stupidity and cowardice make him a mediocre and repulsive figure. Thérèse is disgusted by him.

However, although he seems boring and insignificant when he is alive, he becomes a fearsome figure after his death. Camille haunts Laurent and Thérèse and does not give them a moment's respite: the bite mark he left in Laurent's neck before dying burns continuously, and the two lovers do not get to fulfil the happy plans they made. This horrific suffering later drives them to madness, then to suicide.

MADAME RAQUIN

Madame Raquin, a widow and former shopkeeper, is a possessive mother. She is completely devoted to her son, and is all the more attached to him because as a child he was fragile and needed a lot of care. She is overly protective, and this turns her son into a selfish, mediocre and dependent man.

When her son dies, she no longer has any reason to live. His death even affects her physically, as her limbs become paralysed. She is manipulated by the lovers, and does not suspect their guilt. She even goes as far as to leave her fortune to Thérèse and accept her marriage to Laurent. However, when she discovers the terrible truth, she wants to avenge her son and see that justice is done. Although paralysis stops her from acting, she still manages to take her revenge as Thérèse and Laurent commit suicide.

THE CAT FRANÇOIS

François is a large tabby cat who belongs to Madame Raquin. He can be considered a character in his own right, as he has some human characteristics: he has a man's name and sometimes, for example on Thursday nights, he seems to be the most human character.

As the novel progresses, the cat takes on a particular significance. He is a silent witness to Thérèse and Laurent's relationship, and seems to know a lot about it, looking on with a severe expression:

> "'Do look at François,' Thérèse said to Laurent. 'It's as though he's realised and will recount it all to Camille this evening. Now, that would be funny, if he started talking in the shop one day: he knows some pretty strange tales where we are concerned.' This idea that François might talk amused the young woman in an odd way. Laurent looked at the cat's big green eyes and felt a shiver run over his flesh" (pp. 39-40).

After Camille dies, he seems to haunt the couple: Thérèse becomes superstitious, and Laurent is convinced that the cat is possessed by Camille's ghost. He feels that the animal looks too human and decides that he will have to kill him.

On the brink of madness, Thérèse and Laurent end up believing that the cat has some sort of diabolical power. Laurent can no longer stand having François around, and kills him in front of Madame Raquin, who looks on helplessly.

ANALYSIS

ZOLA: A SCIENTIFIC WRITER

Naturalism

The progress of modern science in the 19th century inspired artists to look at art in a different way. They had the idea of taking techniques and approaches from science in order to produce works that objectively depicted reality.

The fundamental laws applied by naturalist novelists are genetic determinism and social determinism. According to social determinism, an individual's socioeconomic environment has an effect on their character, while genetic determinism suggests that moral and psychological predispositions are passed on from parents to children.

This new genre of novel broke with literary tradition:

- Imagination was replaced by observation and deduction.
- Beautiful subjects were abandoned in favour of reality, and heroes were replaced by ordinary people. Artistic sense was now linked to composition rather than content.
- The plot was no longer determined by moral and social values.

Thérèse Raquin was the first illustration of naturalism in literature. The author described himself as a naturalist writer in the novel's preface. This is indicated by a number of elements:

- **The characters are analysed scientifically.** The characters in the novel are governed by their bodies. Camille leads a mediocre life because he has a frail constitution; Laurent looks for easy, lasting pleasures because of his hot-headed temperament; and Thérèse's nervous character comes from her African heritage and the environment she grew up in ("From the age of ten this woman had been troubled by nervous disorders, partly due to her growing up in the tepid, foul-smelling air of the room where little Camille would be groaning away", p. 138). Psychology therefore depends on physiology.
- **The novel features experimental study.** What will happen if a hot-headed nature and a nervous nature are brought together? In his literary laboratory, Zola set out to conduct an experiment to answer this question. The combination of their two temperaments and the desire to satisfy their physical needs lead Thérèse and Laurent to crime.

Genetic determinism

In the face of the many negative criticisms describing his book as amoral, pornographic and disgusting, Zola explained himself in a preface to the new edition. In it, he confirmed that he had been influenced by science:

> "In *Thérèse Raquin*, I wanted to study temperaments, not characters. [...] I chose characters wholly dominated by their nerves and their blood, devoid of free will, driven to every act in their lives by the fatalities of their flesh [...] It is becoming clear, I hope, that my objective was above all scientific [...] I have tried to explain the strange union that can take

place between two different temperaments, I have shown the profound disturbances of a hot-headed nature in contact with a nervous nature. The reader who reads the novel with care will see that each chapter is the study of a curious case of physiology."[1]

In this preface, Zola stresses his technique as a naturalist author: he claims that he carries out the same analytical work on his characters as a surgeon does on dead bodies. In his novel, the main features of the characters' behaviour are determined by their physical constitution. Here he uses humourism, one of the founding ideas of the medicine of Antiquity. According to this theory, the body is an organism with a certain number of "humours" (blood causes a warm or hot-headed temperament, phlegm causes a weak, apathetic temperament, and so on) which can be balanced or unbalanced.

Each character is predisposed to madness by their physiology. Camille's sickly state – his phlegm – makes him perpetually anxious and dazed. Thérèse, who has a nervous temperament (she is dominated by her nerves, which make her sensitive but also fickle), has a tendency towards hysteria. Her character is also determined by her Algerian blood, which she has inherited from her mother: she feels "a wild desire to run and to shout" (p. 11), has crazy dreams and sometimes lets out a wild, animalistic side. However, most of the time she restrains herself: "inwardly she lived a burning, passionate existence" (ibid.). When she meets Laurent, who is a real man, a sudden and all-consuming passion erupts in

---

1. This quotation has been translated by BrightSummaries.com.

her. She is then like an animal, with no free will, having given in to the movements of her nervous temperament.

Laurent is hot-headed (he is dominated by his blood, which makes him physically strong but morally weak). His hot-headed constitution predisposes him to animal behaviour ("Everything seemed unconscious in that flourishing, animal nature; he obeyed his instincts, he let himself be driven by what his body yearned for", p. 47). Killing Camille changes him: his nerves gain the upper hand over his hot-headed side, he loses his heaviness, and he becomes anxious and afraid.

Zola stated in the preface to the new edition that even remorse is a disorder of the body, as the nervous system rebels against the act that has been committed. For Zola, the soul has no influence; everything is a matter of body and instinct. He was also inspired by the theory of the German philosopher Arthur Schopenhauer (1788-1860), according to which man is subject to desire throughout his entire life. If our desires are not fulfilled, we only experience suffering. Conversely, if they are fulfilled, we will feel genuine satisfaction, but unfortunately this will always be short-lived. Boredom, disgust and even madness always emerge in the end, as is the case for the two lovers.

Scientific writing

The analytical style of the book is expressed in several ways:

- The sentences are short, there is little dialogue and each chapter is brief. The writing style resembles that of a scientific report.

- The semantic field of science is very developed. The vocabulary used is clinical and medical. Some passages are reminiscent of diagnoses.
- Zola aims to describe reality as it is, without embellishing it. To this end, his writing is concrete throughout the story, and he does not shy away from the trivial when describing daily life ("[the group] then repaired to the eating-house, where a table for seven had been laid in a small yellow-painted private room smelling of dust and wine", p. 120).
- The time indicators place events in a linear chronology and give the narrative perfect logical coherence.
- The narrator fades into the background to give the illusion of objectivity. The use of third person pronouns allows the author to give the impression of truth. However, the naturalist novelist does sometimes intervene in the story: objectivity does not exclude all subjectivity.

The fact that the writing is analytical does not make it any less expressive. Zola has a predilection for exaggeration and soundbites. His skill in formulating phrases is admirable.

ELEMENTS OF THE DETECTIVE NOVEL

Although *Thérèse Raquin* is undeniably a naturalist novel, the author gives the reader the illusion that they are reading a detective story.

Far from prying eyes, Laurent pushes Camille into the water and then returns to the boat, before going to look for Camille in order to cover up what he has just done. He delivers a flawless performance and pretends to be upset: "He threw himself into the water, he searched for Camille in the places he could not possibly have been, he came back weeping, twisting his arms, tearing his hair" (p. 66). Thérèse, helped by her natural character, acts out a nervous breakdown. Nobody could ever suspect that they are guilty.

The police botch their investigation. Their friends from Thursday night, the old police commissioner Michaud and his son Olivier, the "chief clerk in the offices of the public order and security police" (p. 19), involuntary help to confirm the verdict of accidental death by presenting Laurent as a brave man who threw himself into the water to save his best friend. Consequently, the two criminals go unpunished. However, this does not stop them from remaining careful and continuing to pretend to be upset.

Their nerves have been stretched to breaking point by the crime, and the precautions they have to take only exacerbate their nervous tension. They end up becoming the victims of their nerves, as they start to suffer from madness, hallucinations, nightmares and terrible anxiety. Laurent and Thérèse wanted to get rid of Camille to remove the obstacle to their relationship, but the spectre of the dead husband drives a wedge between them. They are driven to suicide.

Although Thérèse and Laurent are not condemned by the authorities, as is usually the case in detective novels, they nonetheless condemn themselves: just like in a detective novel, crime does not pay.

APPARENTLY FANTASTIC ELEMENTS

Zola's novel is distinctive because, within his naturalist narrative, the author incorporates elements which seem at first glance to be connected to the fantastic. The fantastic register is characterised by the intrusion of the supernatural into a realistic setting, and this is exactly what happens in *Thérèse Raquin*: strange elements appear in the realistic setting typical of 19th-century fiction, in this case the daily life of the titular character.

For example, the cat is unusual because it seems human. In particular, it seems to understand what is happening in the house. It is a witness to Thérèse and Laurent's adultery and appears as more and more of a threat as the story progresses: it seems to know about the murder. In this sense, it is similar to another famous cat from 19th-century literature, *The Black Cat* (1843) by Edgar Allen Poe (American poet and novelist, 1809-1849).

THE BLACK CAT BY EDGAR ALLEN POE

In this fantastic short story, the narrator is haunted by a cat he has killed. When he adopts another cat, which looks like the old one, he cannot stop thinking about the dead cat. The man eventually tries to kill the new cat as well, but misses and accidentally kills his wife instead. He hides her body in a wall to conceal his crime, but it is found by the police. They are alerted by the cat's wails, since the narrator had also trapped it in the wall without realising.

In both Zola's novel and Poe's short story, the cat represents the protagonists' guilt: the cats seem to haunt them to remind them of their crimes, which will not go unpunished forever. They also represent their madness: it is only the protagonists, eaten away at by their crimes, who see the cats as witnesses and judges of their actions. This interpretation completely removes the fantastic nature of the novel.

The other fantastic element is Laurent's portrait of Camille, which seems to glow with an evil light. It is striking because of its incredible resemblance to its model, but above all because of its sinister appearance which foreshadows his death:

> "The portrait was vile, a dirty grey with broad purple slabs. Laurent could not use the most brilliant colours without rendering them dull and muddy, he had, despite himself, exaggerated his model's deathly pale complexion, and Camille's face was like the greenish visage of a drowned man; the twisted outline convulsed the features, rendering the sinister likeness all the more striking" (p. 32).

The representation of Camille therefore presages his death.

Finally, Camille haunts the lovers after his death:

> "All of a sudden Laurent thought he was having a hallucination. As he turned, coming back to the bed from the window, he saw Camille in a thickly shadowed corner, between the fireplace and the mirrored wardrobe. The face of his victim was green-tinged and distorted, just as he had seen it on the slab on the Morgue. [...]
> 'There, there,' said Laurent in a terrified voice. [...]

> Horror creeping over her, Thérèse came to huddle against him. 'It's his portrait,' she murmured in a low voice, as though her former husband's painted face might have been able to hear her" (p. 131).

At times, Camille even seems to have become a ghost. The two lovers hallucinate, see his face or outline in their bedroom, and witness their bed moving by itself. These visions generally take place at night, which contributes to the development of an atmosphere of terror until the end of the novel. It would therefore seem that the supernatural genuinely intervenes in the couple's life. However, we must remember that these visions are only present in the tortured minds of the lovers, who are increasingly stricken by anguish and paranoia.

In spite of all these fantastic elements, Zola preserves his scientist's instincts and uses nightmarish imagery drawn from the fantastic to describe the behaviour of two characters who are sinking into madness. In reality, these strange phenomena come from the imaginations of Laurent and Thérèse, who are haunted by guilt and remorse.

A NOVEL OF MADNESS

The clash between Thérèse and Laurent's temperaments gradually leads the two protagonists down the path of madness. This slide towards insanity forms the narrative thread of the novel.

Their passionate and feverish affair is the first shock ("He was no longer himself; his mistress [...] had insinuated herself little by little into every fiber of his body", p. 47). Laurent is possessed and Thérèse, who is usually calm and obedient, starts acting like a courtesan after she meets Laurent.

The second shock takes place after the crime. Laurent becomes very anxious as his nerves gain the upper hand over his blood. He becomes less calm and unflinching, and his mind and body are wracked by anxiety. Thérèse, for her part, goes through several stages: joy, remorse, nervous breakdowns and vague reveries.

Married life completes this descent into madness. The mere presence of the other person reminds both of them of their crime, and every night is torture ("So like two enemies who had been tied together and were making vain efforts to escape from this forced coupling, they strained their muscles and their nerves, tensing themselves without managing to break free. [...] And so they lived in a state of chronic exasperation, tired of themselves, unable to endure a word, a gesture, a look without suffering and raving", p. 178). They mistrust one another and both live in fear that the other person will reveal everything; consequently, Thérèse and Laurent end up hating one another ("This was an atrocious hate, marked by dreadful explosions. They were well aware that they were constricting each other, they kept telling themselves that they would be living in peace if they were not always here, face to face", p. 177).

Their situation is unbearable, and they both have the idea of killing the other person at the same time. However, their constant mistrust stops them from carrying this out ("At that instant, the strange sensation which warns of the approach of danger made the couple turn around in one instinctive movement. They looked at each other: Thérèse saw the flask in Laurent's hands, and Laurent caught sight of the white flash of the knife that glistened between the folds of Thérèse's skirts", p. 215). They end up committing suicide, the only way of escaping their suffering.

A SCANDALOUS BOOK

Thérèse Raquin was one of Zola's first novels. In it, the author laid the foundations of his theory of naturalism, which broke with traditional literature. It is therefore unsurprising that the book was shocking when it was first published. The journalist Louis Ulbach (1822-1889), who wrote under the pen name Ferragus, denounced the beginnings of naturalism in his 1868 *Le Figaro* article "La littérature putride" ("Putrid literature"). He wrote of "a monstrous school of novelists, who seek to substitute the elegance of the charnel house for the elegance of the flesh, who appeal to the most surgical curiosities, who bring together the plague-stricken so that the reader may admire the sores"[2]. In the same article, he attacked *Thérèse Raquin*: "This book summarises all the putridness of contemporary literature too faithfully to avoid arousing anger. It is not the result of an individual fancy, but of a contagion which infects all our literature". In response, Zola wrote in the same newspaper that novelists should not feel indebted to the public, and should be free to examine human nature as they saw fit.

---

2. All quotations from Ulbach's article have been translated by BrightSummaries.com.

Through naturalism, Zola sought to scientifically examine human behaviour. In *Thérèse Raquin*, he demonstrates the reaction caused by the encounter of two beings, one governed by their nerves and the other by their blood.

FURTHER REFLECTION

SOME QUESTIONS TO THINK ABOUT...

- Why can Thérèse be described as the main character of the novel? Justify your answer.
- In what ways does Zola apply genetic and social determinism to his characters?
- Are Thérèse and Laurent heroes? Justify your answer.
- Compare *Thérèse Raquin* with the novels in Balzac's *La Comédie humaine* ("The Human Comedy"). Do the two novelists share a similar goal? Justify your answer.
- At times the novel seems to contain fantastic elements. Explain what they are and why they feature in the story.
- Do you think Zola's vision of humanity is realistic?
- What methods does the author use to make his novel as objective as possible?
- In what ways does this novel prefigure the *Les Rougon-Macquart* cycle?
- Do the film adaptations of *Thérèse Raquin* manage to convey the objectivity and scientific aspect of Zola's novel?
- Do you think that the ending of this novel is worthy of a tragedy?

We want to hear from you!
Leave a comment on your online library
and share your favourite books on social media!

FURTHER READING

REFERENCE EDITION

- Zola, É. (2013) *Thérèse Raquin*. Trans. Thorpe, A. London: Vintage.

REFERENCE STUDIES

- Horne, E. (2016) *Zola and the Victorians: Censorship in the Age of Hypocrisy*. London: MacLehose Press.
- Nelson, B. (2007) *The Cambridge Companion to Zola*. Cambridge: Cambridge University Press.
- Schom, A. (1987) *Emile Zola: A Biography*. London: Queen Anne Press.

ADAPTATIONS

- *Thérèse Raquin*. (1911) [Film]. Einar Zangenberg. Dir. Denmark.
- *Thérèse Raquin*. (1915) [Film]. Nino Martoglio. Dir. Italy: Milano Film, Morgana Films.
- *Thérèse Raquin*. (1928) [Film]. Jacques Feyder. Dir. France/Germany: Deutsche Film Union.
- *Thérèse Raquin*. (1953) [Film]. Marcel Carné. Dir. France/Italy: Paris Film Productions, Lux Films.

MORE FROM BRIGHTSUMMARIES.COM

- Reading guide – *L'Assommoir* by Émile Zola.
- Reading guide – *Nana* by Émile Zola.

- Reading guide – *The Belly of Paris* by Émile Zola.
- Reading guide – *The Earth* by Émile Zola.
- Reading guide – *The Fortune of the Rougons* by Émile Zola.
- Reading guide – *The Ladies' Paradise* by Émile Zola.

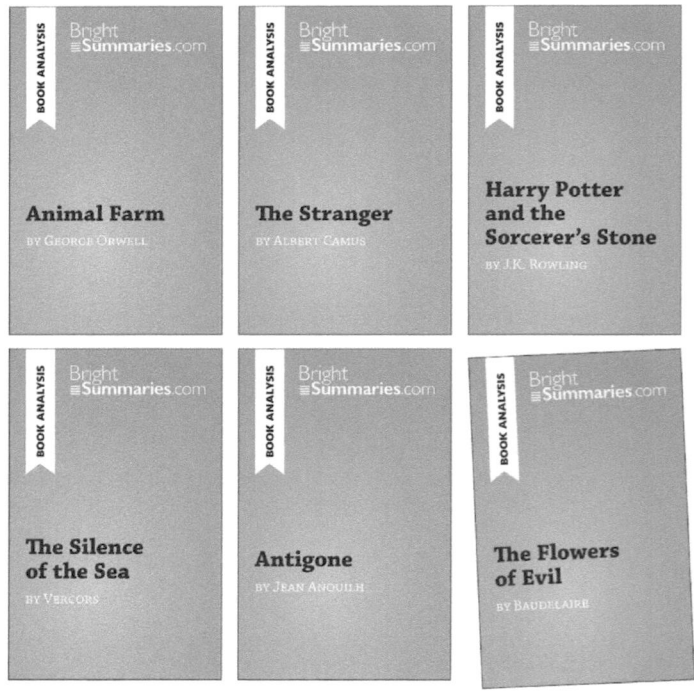

www.brightsummaries.com

Ebook EAN: 9782806295620

Paperback EAN: 9782806297297

Legal Deposit: D/2017/12603/261

This guide was written with the collaboration of Pauline Coullet for the analysis of the cat François and the chapters 'Genetic determinism', 'Scientific writing', 'Apparently fantastic elements' and 'A scandalous book'.

Cover: © Primento

Digital conception by Primento, the digital partner of publishers.

This guide was produced with the support of the *Service Général des Lettres et du Livre* of the Wallonia-Brussels Federation.